We Clea

by Ellen Dalton
illustrated by Laura Ovresat

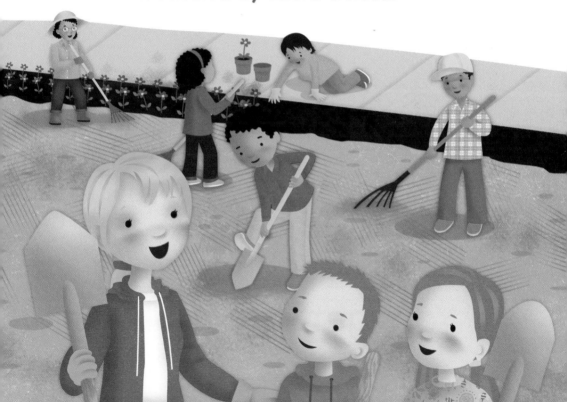

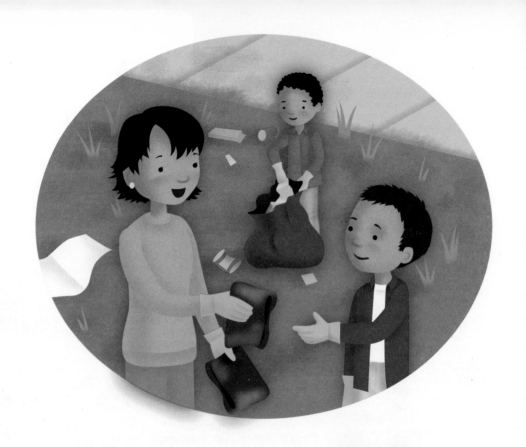

You get the 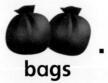.

bags

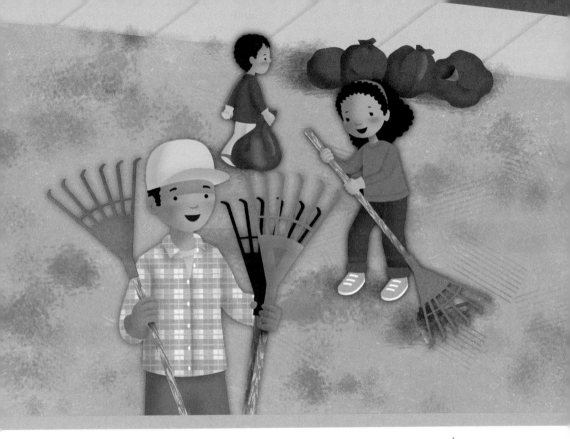

You get the 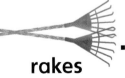.

rakes

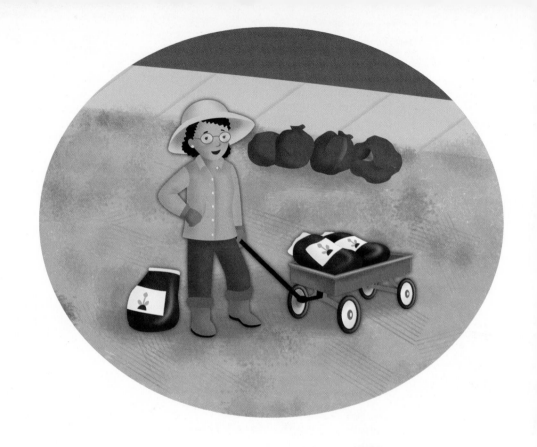

You get the .
dirt

4

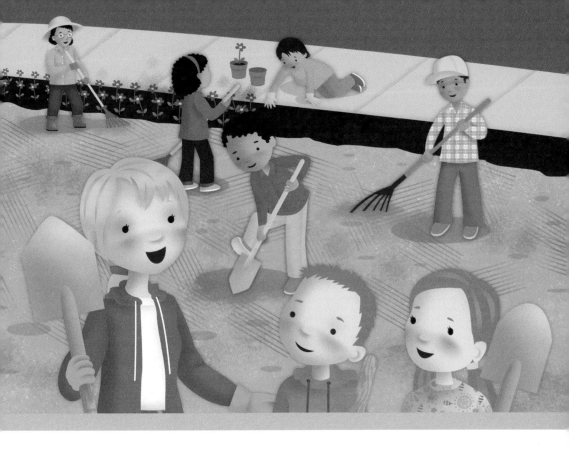

You get the 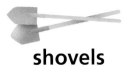.

shovels

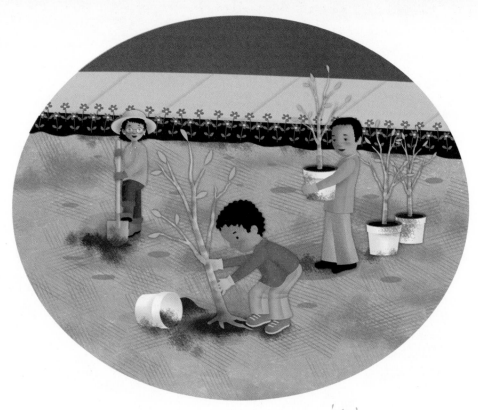

You get the .
trees

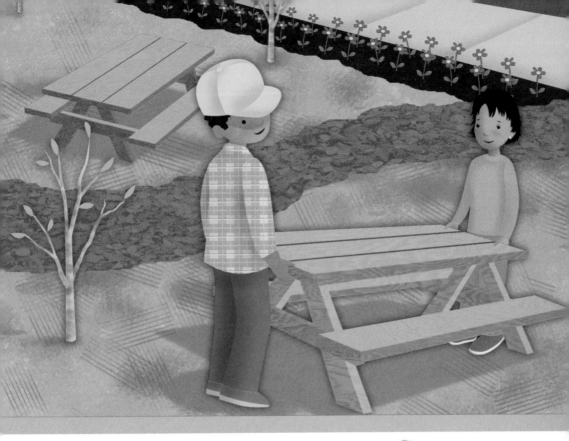

You get the .

table

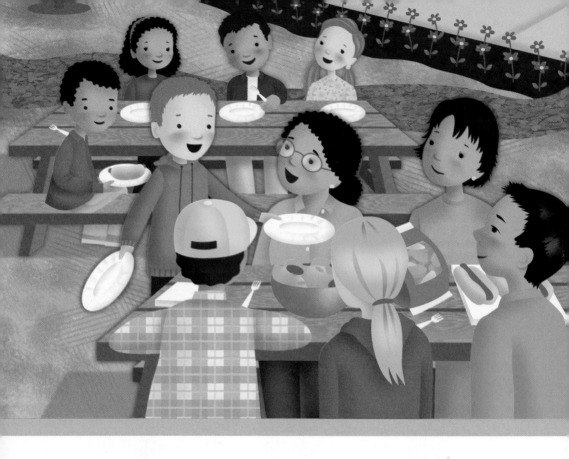

You get the 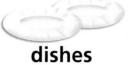.

dishes